Pearls For The Bride

Laura Thomas

For Robin~
congratulations!
Blessings & Joy!

ALL RIGHTS RESERVED
No part of this book may be reproduced or transmitted in any form or by any means, electronic or mechanical, including photocopying, recording, or by any information storage and retrieval system, without permission in writing from the author, except in the case of brief quotations embodied in reviews.

Cover Art: Val Muller

Copyright ©Laura Thomas 2014
All rights reserved
ISBN 13: 978-0692213667
ISBN 10: 069221366X

DWB PUBLISHING
www.dancingwithbearpublishing.com

Foreword

This is merely a letter—albeit a rather long letter. A few pearls of wisdom for the new bride.

Specifically, to my beautiful, brilliant, feisty, loving daughter, as you embark upon this exciting journey of marriage — I have much to tell you. So much, in fact, that the letter became a book, and I hope and pray it will be beneficial to you and any other new brides who may happen across its pages. This is written from a woman's perspective — a wife with a great deal yet to learn, but a desire to share as much as possible with you right now, at the cusp of the journey with your wonderful husband-to-be.

As we celebrated our twenty-fifth wedding anniversary this year, it felt right to pour out my heart at this time. I'm no marriage expert with academic letters trailing my name, but I know how it feels to be cherished within a marriage and to love the same man fiercely for many, many years. What I know, I share willingly. And I know for a fact that without God at the center of our marriage, we would be shipwrecked. He is our foundation, our hope — and He is yours, too.

My prayer is that you will be encouraged, excited, and edified by these "pearls" as you dig deeper into life as a new wife. Marriage is a crazy adventure, and you're about to set sail on the wildest, most glorious seas imaginable...

Love always,
Mum x

Table of Contents:

Chapter One:
Que Sera Surreal

Dear Daughter,

As I write this book with you, my grown-up little girl in mind, I also write to other daughters out there... all those who are newly wed or preparing to be a bride. Join me, lovely young ladies, as we dive in and see what pearls of wisdom we can dig up and ponder...

> *"When I was just a little girl*
> *I asked my mother, what will I be*
> *Will I be pretty, will I be rich*
> *Here's what she said to me*
>
> *Que Sera, Sera,*
> *Whatever will be, will be*
> *The future's not ours, to see*
> *Que Sera, Sera*
> *What will be, will be"*
> (*Que Sere, Sera* Jay Livingston & Ray Evens, 1956, original artist Doris Day)

Do you remember when you were a little girl? You had big dreams for your future, even from an early age. You were the quintessential girly girl, refusing to wear trousers until you turned seven. Frilly dresses, dollhouses, your big plastic kitchen — it was a mass of pink and pretty.

11

When I watched you, I wondered about your future, and it was surreal. I couldn't imagine you all grown up with a career and a husband, and one day, children of your own. But then again, maybe I *could* picture it, a glimpse at least. I knew you would be passionate about whatever cause you followed — I could see that by your intensity even in play. I knew you would be caring and loving from the way you love-smothered your puppy. You were scarily smart from the beginning, and I soon realized school would be a breeze for you, and you would pursue more and more knowledge, eating it up with a ravenous appetite.

And now, here you are. The years shaped you and grew you into a beautiful bride-to-be. All the *dream wedding* files and spreadsheets you created since the age of twelve were virtual stepping-stones to your very own *Big Day*. You will feel like a princess. How many times did you watch *Cinderella* as a little one, enraptured by the girl in rags being swept off her feet by her Prince Charming? And now it's your turn — for real. Minus the rags.

Your wedding day will be spectacular. In answer to the *Que Sera* song, yes — you will be pretty (massive understatement), and you will be rich (even if just for the day, and thereafter you will find riches in so many areas of life.) Every eye will be on you, and all your loved ones will wish you the happiest of everything for the rest of your lives.

But what happens after the nuptial cake is consumed?

Yes, your wedding day is hugely important. It will be unique, gorgeous, and unquestionably the biggest whirlwind of your life thus far. But it's only the beginning. Every betrothed couple will put a great deal of time and attention into planning a *wedding*, but is a proportionate amount of time spent planning the *marriage*? For most of us, probably not nearly enough time, if we're being completely honest. It's like going on a luxurious cruise and only packing an outfit for the first day. Some people can live like that, throwing caution to the wind and singing, "Whatever will be, will be..." but surely intelligent packing and planning is the way to go.

Be prepared for every kind of weather on your love boat, dear daughter. Know where the life vests are kept for when you need to keep each other afloat, make sure there's room for you both to pursue your passions onboard (because this is one *very* long cruise), and confirm you are both comfortable with the stops en route as well as the destination... these details are rather essential. And best to be organized *before* you set sail.

Most of us are familiar with the "Proverbs 31 wife". Love her or loathe her, she is recorded right there in Scripture. Some women see her as an unrealistic example, a wonder woman of yesteryear penned to shine a light on our inadequacies. But I like her. A lot. And I think she has many pearls of wisdom for us. Her description is a hefty load to take in at one sitting, so we'll look in on her attributes a little more throughout this book, but here's the complete lowdown:

"The Wife of Noble Character
A wife of noble character who can find?
She is worth far more than rubies.
Her husband has full confidence in her
and lacks nothing of value.
She brings him good, not harm,
all the days of her life.

She selects wool and flax
and works with eager hands.
She is like the merchant ships,
bringing her food from afar.
She gets up while it is still night;
she provides food for her family
and portions for her female servants.
She considers a field and buys it;
out of her earnings she plants a vineyard.
She sets about her work vigorously;
her arms are strong for her tasks.
She sees that her trading is profitable,
and her lamp does not go out at night.
In her hand she holds the distaff
and grasps the spindle with her fingers.
She opens her arms to the poor
and extends her hands to the needy.
When it snows, she has no fear for her household;
for all of them are clothed in scarlet.
She makes coverings for her bed;
she is clothed in fine linen and purple.
Her husband is respected at the city gate,
where he takes his seat among the elders of the
land.
She makes linen garments and sells them,
and supplies the merchants with sashes.
She is clothed with strength and dignity;
she can laugh at the days to come.
She speaks with wisdom,
and faithful instruction is on her tongue.
She watches over the affairs of her household
and does not eat the bread of idleness.
Her children arise and call her blessed;
her husband also, and he praises her:
'Many women do noble things,
but you surpass them all.'

Charm is deceptive, and beauty is fleeting;
but a woman who fears the LORD is to be
praised.
Honor her for all that her hands have done,
and let her works bring her praise at the city
gate."
Proverbs 31:10-31 (NIV)

I don't know what your deep thoughts are on the word *wife*, but after reading this passage, I'm hit with: *confident, strong, industrious, respected, businesswoman, caring, multi-tasker extraordinaire, entrepreneur, compassionate, mother, intelligent, well-dressed, energetic,* and *priceless*. There is nothing timid, unbecoming, or weak about this woman, and we need to bear that in mind as we consider "wifeliness".

Twenty-five years ago, I couldn't imagine what it would feel like to be a "real wife". I was super young, super naïve, and all I knew was that I loved my fiancé and couldn't wait until I was married. I was living the dream. But I couldn't picture what being married would look like on a daily basis. I'm not a worrier by nature, so it didn't exactly keep me up at night, but I pondered, and it might concern you somewhat. Will you be a good wife? Will he be a good husband? What *is* a good wife? How will you know if you're doing everything right? Will your husband even know the difference?

I'll let you into a little secret: in the beginning, none of us know how to be a good wife. None of us could imagine ourselves throwing a dinner party or throwing a tantrum, depending on the day. We've never had to wash male underwear before or explain the amount of chocolate in our secret stash. What will all this stuff look like?

The good news is, our little song from the beginning of this chapter is quite correct when it says "the future's not ours to see". That's probably just as well, all things considered. There is only One who sees what is lying ahead for us — in our marriage and in every aspect of our lives.

"I make known the end from the beginning, from ancient times, what is still to come. I say, 'My purpose will stand, and I will do all that I please.'"
Isaiah 46:10 (NIV)

God is the Alpha and Omega, the beginning and the end. He knows all and He sees all. He knew you when you were a little girl, and He sees you now at the start of this new chapter of your life. Fret not. You don't need to know all the details and have plans ready for the next fifty years, and you don't need spreadsheets detailing your evening meals for the next decade. Seriously, there's planning and there's *crazy* planning.

Take a breath — you're going on a lifetime cruise, full of highs and lows and everything in between, with your Prince Charming. You can't see what is going to happen next week or next year, and you don't actually need to. This is fresh and exciting and new. Surreal? Yes. Scary? Maybe. An adventure? Like no other. Trust God, both of you. Together.

"Trust in the LORD with all your heart
and lean not on your own understanding;
in all your ways submit to him,
and he will make your paths straight."
Proverbs 3:5-6 (NIV)

Chapter Two:
In The Beginning...

Apparently, back in the day, the Greeks believed pearls would promote marital harmony and even prevent newlywed brides from crying. I adore pearls whatever their function, and love that even today, they are a popular choice for brides. However, I certainly wouldn't rely on your jewelry to get you through the beginning of your marriage. The pearls in this book are offered as words of hope, encouragement, advice and inspiration. Little pearls of wisdom. So we'll start in the beginning.

As I'm sure you are aware, dear daughter, there are some who treat the first year of marriage like a prison sentence of sorts. "We made it through unscathed." "It was the hardest year of my life." "If I'd known what it would be like, I may have had second thoughts." Wow. There's still confetti in the suitcase and feelings of failure and thoughts of escape are rampant. Are there really divorces after only one year of marriage?

Granted, there is a great deal of adjustment required to meld two separate lives into one. It really depends on who is willing to roll their newly wed sleeves up and give the relationship the attention it needs. You *could* declare "love conquers all" and bury your head in the sand, hoping your deep love for your husband will cover a multitude of discrepancies. But, like anything else, if you want the very best outcome, it's going to take a good chunk of effort from you both.

The Bible actually underlines this premise way back in the Old Testament, when instructions were given for the newlywed man:

"If a man has recently married, he must not be sent to war or have any other duty laid on him. For one year he is to be free to stay at home and bring happiness to the wife he has married." Deuteronomy 24:5 (NIV)

I love this verse! It gives credence to working on a marriage relationship, especially in the early days. "For one year..." Surely that first year of marriage is vital. It's a time of adaptation and growth, where fertile ground for love in the relationship can be solidified, cemented, and set as a foundation to build on thereafter.

The problem is, we are a people of instant gratification. If something looks shabby, we get a new one; if something looks saggy, we get it lifted. We don't like to be patient, work hard at things, tough it out. We enjoy everything in "click-of-a-mouse" time. But this new place you're in, this being half of a whole suddenly, it's tricky business — but it's also God-ordained and glorious, and thoroughly worth every minute spent nurturing it.

This number one year, when you're both on tender hooks just a little, almost waiting for some nasty habit to reveal itself or some blast from the past to rock your wedded bliss, this is when you need your champagne glass to be 'half full'.

You could sing the *half-empty-woe-is-me* song, focusing on everything you are *not* anymore. You are not single, you cannot think only of yourself and relish making decisions based on you and you alone, and you probably shouldn't leave your make-up and hair paraphernalia strewn all over the sink claiming the entire bathroom territory. He may need a spot for his toothbrush or something.

You have the option to choose the half-full version. You are *married,* you have someone special to come home to each night, you need never feel lonely, you have someone to share your every joy, pain, laughter, and tears with twenty-four hours a day if necessary (lucky him). You have a partner for life, a very best friend, and your very own family.

Yes, there will be newness to get used to at first. I clearly remember your father and my honeymoon in Cyprus, and how I would wake up early (you know how ridiculous and completely uncharacteristic that is), and scurry into the bathroom to brush my teeth. Why? So my new husband could wake up to my fresh, minty breath, of course. I had placed rather high expectations on myself, and quite honestly, it didn't last long once I realized he didn't pay much heed to morning breath. I think I persevered for a week, and then relaxed once I discovered the absurdity of my paranoia.

Relax.

This is brand new for both of you. You get to be yourself all of the time, warts and all, and so does he. That comes with a plethora of quirks and peculiarities, but the sooner you embrace them, the easier it will be. Remember, you didn't marry your beloved in order to change him. If you think of it as a fresh, exciting experience, you will obviously enjoy the ride a lot more. The first year is the marriage learning curve at its most severe, but with a sense of humor, a good dose of patience, some give and take, and a healthy perspective on everything you do together, you have the potential to flourish.

19

"There is no place like home."
(L. Frank Baum, *The Wonderful Wizard of Oz*.)

One aspect to get used to together is your new dwelling place — be it apartment, house, dorm, or shed. You both *need* a sanctuary to call home. It will be the nest where you are completely comfortable, able to relax, and put your own special mark upon. It's a refuge where you will grow together and make unique memories as newlyweds.

Your first home will probably not be your dream home, but that doesn't mean you can't make it special. Your dad and I started in a tiny apartment in Wales — a third floor slice of ancient house with drafty windows and a spectacular sea view. We paid peanuts for rent, and knew it was a temporary arrangement, so we determined to enjoy it.

We braved the elements regularly climbing that fire escape to get in and out of our cozy little flat. I actually dropped a fridge on my new husband once when we were trying to carry it down those iron steps. We laughed a lot in our first home. Especially at my cooking (I didn't know you couldn't grill carrots), regularly watching our guests gradually slump onto the living room floor because our funky futon was lacking in substance, and we were parenting our little kitten. Good times.

We scrimped and saved until we had enough to put a deposit down on a "real" house, but our pre-mortgage days were somewhat carefree, fun, and a time we wouldn't trade for anything. I got terribly creative with swags of Laura Ashley fabric purchased on sale, (even our Proverbs 31 wife made "coverings for her bed") and I melded our tastes, finding a rhythm to our décor likes and dislikes.

Sometimes give and take and a little compromise are required (and I'm still finding that out twenty-five years later), but there's something very gratifying about working on your space together and seeing a little of each of you reflected in your surroundings. Make it somewhere you both *want* to come home to after a really long day, and enjoy your home.

It worries me when I see a young bride desperately wanting to go back home with alarming regularity. She feels the need to be back in her familiar, pre-married surroundings with parents and siblings for a "home fix". Not that the relationship with your loved ones should be severed, not at all, but it should change. It's the essential "leave" part of the "leave and cleave" mentioned in the Bible — it's near impossible to do the cleaving unless you have effectively done the leaving.

Your comfort now is in your new home with your new husband, and unless you are able to fully commit by putting 100% into this next step geographically (even if it's only down the street), then you will put yourself through a lot of heartache. Not to mention your poor spouse. Like everything else, it works both ways, so, similarly, he shouldn't go scurrying back for his mom's pot-roast every day instead of coming home to you in your new place. Go back home together for pot-roast with the family and enjoy some catching up time, but I would strongly advise it not to become a daily occurrence.

Your family will either make this transition to being a wife easier or an absolute nightmare. As I write this with you, my daughter, in mind, I truly hope we will be the former! Twenty-five years ago, we were blessed as newlyweds with very nonintrusive, supportive family on both sides, but I know from friends who have been through the aforementioned nightmare, that is not always the case. Some families, or even friends, will make it their sole purpose in life to 'be there' for you in the early days of your marriage, and I don't mean in a good way. They will literally 'be there', right in your new home on your new couch, way too regularly and completely unannounced, determined to keep you company and make sure you are adjusting okay.

They will pounce on even the slightest sigh passing your lips and 'be there' in a flash as your counselor, or worse, as your escape route. Quite often, they are well-meaning. They think they are helping, when in reality they are hindering you from growing into your new role. You might want to take a stand before any real damage is done and graciously ask them to back off.

My final piece of advice on year number one is to plan a vacation. It might feel as if your honeymoon just tapped out your vacation budget for the next decade, but I believe there's some merit to taking some time out for the two of you after a year of change and acclimatization.

Look at a destination that's going to be fun and stress-free (cash permitting of course). After our first year of marriage, I got a 'bee in my bonnet' about us going to Disneyworld. It was probably something psychologically deep, like reclaiming my childhood after getting married relatively young, but I simply wanted to do Disney, which seemed a million miles away from our lives in the U.K. So, while the new husband was out playing soccer one morning, I did all the groundwork (not easy back in the day before online everything) and put the wheels in motion for visiting Mickey. On arriving home, he was greatly surprised with my ingenious idea, and once I got the grin of approval, we were booked. It was the most frivolous, childlike two weeks in Florida imaginable, and worth every single penny. Sometimes you have to go all out in the name of fun and memory making. But if the purse strings are tightly pinched, get creative and find your own "Disneyworld", even if it's for a long weekend or in a tent!

Chapter Three:
Cruise Or Shipwreck?

"She is clothed with strength and dignity; she can laugh at the days to come."

Oh, daughter, if only life could be plain sailing! You haven't been raised in a plastic bubble, so you are more than aware that each day, month or year has its up's and down's. It's how we learn, stretch ourselves, and grow. As Christians, we know to look to God for guidance and strength through the 'lows' and remember to be utterly thankful through the 'highs', but sometimes it's tough, and sometimes we're too wrapped up in ourselves to involve Him in the process at all. But I want to offer some words of encouragement to you in these early days as a brand new wife, as you embark upon your adventure of a lifetime, and *for* a lifetime.

I can't help thinking of marriage as a voyage. It's like a sailing expedition of epic proportions with smooth seas and spectacular sunsets, but always the threat of storms lurking on the horizon. There will doubtless be both extremes for you, and you will learn to appreciate the luxury of still waters once you've come through and survived the eye of the storm.

"I'm not afraid of storms, for I'm learning to sail my ship." (Aeschylus)

It's all in the sailing. The how's and when's and where's. Some of us are better equipped than others to be willing to learn the ropes and be prepared. Let's talk literally here for a moment. My darling husband's passion for sailing his catamaran is no secret. He lights up when he sniffs a breeze in the air, and being out on the lake is his happy place. He took sailing lessons and knows his way around every inch of that little boat. I, on the other hand, am a little less sailing savvy. I enjoy floating out on the lake with a good book and the sun on my shoulders, but I have zero interest in *how* I get out there. Probably not smart, and I do occasionally wonder what would happen if he fell in and hit his head, and I was left to save the day. Scary thought. My plan is to scream until someone comes to our rescue, but the point is, it's prudent to be prepared to carry one another through the blustery gales of life. Learning to sail our love boat is an art and takes some practice. And even then we can get sloppy and make some harrowing mistakes en route.

Chances are, you will have a very different coping mechanism from your husband. It's common to find one stress-ball married to a chilled-out individual. Depending on the extremes, it can work very well. Case in point, your father needs me to calm him down regularly and put everything in perspective, while I need him to keep us all afloat and wear the sensible head. We drive each other undeniably crazy on occasion, but at the end of the day, we *know* we need each other and we *know* we are a sailing crew working together with the same destination on the map.

When it comes to weathering storms, I don't want to paint a horrific picture for you, young newlywed with high hopes and expectations. In fact, I'd like to dwell for a moment on the true 'wedded bliss' periods, because they are worth basking in.

25

There will be beautiful times ahead for you and your husband. You will lie on your loungers on the top deck, taking in the sun and enjoying the cruise immensely. I get a little frustrated when books and blogs and articles forget to mention the golden moments. We see plenty of marriage failure fodder out there, but there is so much to be said about the wonder of being wed.

Marriage is a "God thing", without a shadow of a doubt. It's not a fad or a cultural institution, and it's nothing new. Way back in the Garden of Eden, God Himself saw that man was lonely and needed someone — a wife. He created her with loving attention to detail, and then Genesis 2 verse 24 says these famous words:

"Therefore shall a man leave his father and his mother, and shall cleave unto his wife: and they shall be one flesh." (KJV)

I particularly like how the King James Version puts it, using the word '"cleave". Other versions say "is united", "hold fast to", or "be joined". But cleaving seems so much deeper somehow. It means to adhere firmly and closely, or loyally and unwaveringly; to come or be in close contact with; stick or hold together and resist separation.

Did you see that? "resist separation". Once you are joined together as man and wife, it feels good and right to be together. Physical separation feels wrong and foreign, even for a short while. We touched a little in the last chapter about leaving the family physically when you are married, and now you cleave to your man, sometimes for dear life, and he cleaves to you in mutual adoration. Those cruise times, when the sun is shining and the storms feel very, very far away — enjoy them. They are a blessing, so be thankful and savor each second. Relish the laughter, tuck away the priceless memories you are making, and don't swindle yourself out of enjoying the joy while you wait for the other shoe to drop.

That other shoe might not fall for years, and when it does, when the storm hits and your boat is rocked, be sure to be close by your husband, because you will need each other desperately. If you can build on your relationship during the calm, you will be better prepared to weather the rough.

On some occasions, the storm might be worse for one of you. Oh, the circumstance will affect you both to some extent, but *you* might feel the brunt of the force and need to hit the deck while *he* grabs a bucket and methodically rids the sinking boat of water. And it will happen vice versa, too, like a 'support tag team'. It may be physical, emotional, spiritual, financial, or a cocktail mix of them all.

If your relationship is ship-shape, you will be sensitive to one another's needs and actually *want* to be there for one another. Your early married months and years are a great training ground for later on when you two become three, or four, or eight. Because, trust me, you'll need to finely tune that 'support tag team' to even survive!

Here's the good news: as Christians, you don't have to brave any storms on your own, or even as a couple.

"We have an anchor that keeps the soul
Steadfast and sure while the billows roll,
Fastened to the Rock which cannot move,
Grounded firm and deep in the Savior's love."

(Words: Priscilla J. Owens, Music: William J. Kirkpatrick)

Our anchor is Jesus. Hebrews 6:19 starts: "We have this hope as an anchor for the soul, firm and secure." (NIV) Deep down, we all crave stability. From an early age, we are comforted by the knowledge that we are safe, and that there is someone greater who will hold us securely throughout the storm. Jesus is our Hope, our Anchor, and our Rock. He's the reason your parents personally have survived through every tough time these past twenty-five years. I know there are successful marriages without God at the helm, but here's the thing about having Jesus as your anchor — there is *nothing* that will ever uproot Him. He is solid and sure, He is God omnipotent. If you both have Him as the very foundation in your relationship and fix your eyes on Him always, it will not crumble. I'm not saying Jesus will make everything rosy, because that's not how it works. The difference is, He will walk with you and show you how to survive and live life to the fullest, even through the rough weather.

Remember our Proverbs 31 woman? I'll bet she had her fair share of storms. She had a family to raise, a business to contend with, and was highly respected in her community. She chose not to spend her time worrying about what might or might not happen to rock her boat. She wasn't consumed with anxiety thinking how everything could fall around her like a stack of cards. This woman was strong. Not an obnoxious strong, but a godly strong. And this, dear daughter, is how we should handle the storms:

"She is clothed with strength and dignity; she can laugh at the days to come." (Proverbs 31:25)

How, you may ask? How did she have strength, dignity, and the ability to laugh at the future? How can *we*? Not on our own, that's for sure:

"The LORD gives strength to his people; the LORD blesses his people with peace." (Psalm 29:11)

For when we trust our Anchor, our Jesus, with any peril looming on the horizon, we can live confidently and joyfully. We can be prepared for the storm without living in its shadow every day, anticipating a shipwreck of monster proportions. And we get to rest in Him, to enjoy the calm waters and share them with our man. Don't fret about the shipwreck and the storms, dear daughter, open your hands and your heart, and enjoy the cruise:

"Do not be anxious about anything, but in everything, by prayer and petition, with thanksgiving, present your requests to God. And the peace of God, which transcends all understanding, will guard your hearts and your minds in Christ Jesus." Philippians 4:6-7 (NIV)

Chapter Four:
Hot Date Husband

"An anniversary is a time to celebrate the joys of today, the memories of yesterday, and the hopes of tomorrow."

"You're positively glowing with love."
"You must be newlyweds."
"Oh, you're still in the honeymoon phase."

Brace yourself, sweet girl, because you'll hear that — a lot, especially the first few weeks and months after your wedding. There's nothing wrong with people seeing how in love you are and how marriage is everything you hoped it would be. Revel in it. Enjoy it while you can, before the skeptics in the peanut gallery start taking aim.

The lead up to your wedding, apart from the obvious stresses and near nervous-breakdown moments, are largely a period of romance. Engagement is a precious time spent dreaming, planning, getting to know each other more, and creating a future map, even if it's a bit fuzzy in places. It's a relatively short period given its importance. Admittedly, some have longer engagements, but for most couples, it's a year, tops. We can't bear to wait a minute longer. Lots of dinner dates, coffee dates, communication, and intentional one-on-one time dedicated to your husband-to-be, and that is as it should be. Well done.

Then the wedding itself is one gigantic date day, wrapped in white and romance and love and vows. The dress, the veil, the covenants made, the flowers, the dancing, the kisses. All of it makes for the ultimate date — even for guests, it's a chance to hold the hand of a loved one a little tighter, remembering vows made years ago, or dreaming of a day exactly like this in the future. Sigh.

But what about after the confetti settles?

I can't stress this enough: *DATE YOUR MAN.* The 'glow' takes work to maintain, and a lot of the work is actually a great deal of fun. Dating. Simple, right?

It may seem like a no-brainer for you at this moment. You have been in dating mode for years, maybe you're fresh off your honeymoon, and it feels like life is one long string of dates. But it won't always be like that. Pretty soon, you'll fall into a much-needed routine. It may even be a relief after the rollercoaster you've been on in the lead up to marriage. You'll both have responsibilities with work or studies, and a home to maintain, maybe even a lawn to mow or a dog to walk — regular stuff. You'll have new friend groups, new church circles, new relationships, and quite frankly, it can be exhausting. You have your man at home, and you are relaxing into a nice, comfortable rhythm, the wedding pressure is off.

These are all good things. I know you will embrace fresh challenges and try to juggle many of them in those newlywed delicate hands of yours, the sparkly wedding band shining bright and clear. But in all the newness, don't lose sight of dating your husband. That young man who walked you out of the church as his wife, needs to be dated *evermore*.

Don't cut him off now, at the cusp of when you start making good habits and beautiful traditions. Don't cut him off later, when you suddenly find yourself knee-deep in diapers and soothers. Don't cut him off when your teenaged kids need you as chauffeur and psychiatrist. Because, if you do, one day in the distant future, when it's just the two of you again, you might have forgotten how to date altogether, and you will have missed a lifetime of special, vital dating memories.

Be spontaneous. It's a scary notion for some, but it works wonders. Surprise him with a special candle-lit dinner 'just because'. Make his favorite dessert and go eat it under the stars on a balmy evening. Get tickets for a movie or sporting event he loves. Go for a walk in the snow and come home for hot chocolate in front of the fire— guys are generally low maintenance and appreciate the most basic of dates, especially the free ones.

Please, *please,* don't ever use money (or lack thereof) as an excuse to not date each other. I'm going to throw it out there that the majority of newly weds are cash-shy. Either very young, fresh out of school with a mountain of student loans, or simply *regular people*. Most start their marriage on a budget. We did, and I wouldn't swap those crazy penny-pinching days for all the tea in China. It's a growing experience like none other — you learn to be resourceful, creative, and content. Oh, it will probably be the root of many an argument, but you'll work through it together. Walks on the beach, sledding, sharing dessert, hiking in the countryside, watching old movies, making a homemade dinner together — these things are virtually costless and completely priceless.

"An anniversary is a time to celebrate the joys of today, the memories of yesterday, and the hopes of tomorrow." (Author Unknown)

A word of caution, and this will probably *not* be applicable to you, dear daughter. You might want to subtly pass this page over to your other half for a quick tip:

Do not *ever* forget your wedding anniversary!

You might wonder how this could ever come to pass, you newlyweds with confetti still in your hair. But for whatever reason, it can be forgotten, and this is not a good scene. Ever. And I hate to generalize, but I will — it's usually the poor husband. Sorry, but it is what it is. We all know some poor guy who has had an unfortunate memory lapse and ended up in the doghouse, his wife bitterly disappointed and cut to the core. I'm sure it happens the other way around too, but I honestly have never heard about it—just saying. If he needs a reminder, for goodness sake remind him, but don't let the special date slip by unnoticed.

I don't speak from experience here. I was a smart young thing and decided to get married the day after my birthday. Thus, my anniversary has never been forgotten because it's somewhat of a double-whammy. Okay, plus I'm one to get rather excited about any and every celebration and there is a 'lead up' period. Regardless, I can't imagine him ever forgetting our wedding anniversary, simply because it's special to him, too.

We have remembered every single one for the past twenty-five years, and I think it's a perfect opportunity to celebrate your love for one another and acknowledge another year together. Our celebrations have been anything from intimate dinners in Welsh restaurants, several years of candle-lit anniversary meals at home once the babies were tucked into bed, a few where we raised our glasses in Hawaii, many in various favorite eating places in our hometown, Kelowna, B.C., and then the latest at a stunning table for two on a beach in St. Lucia for our twenty-fifth. Each one special in its own way — each one giving undivided attention to our spouse. I can't imagine ever "forgetting" to celebrate. Please, please don't ever forget.

One last little pearl — did you notice how pretty much everything awesome revolves around food? There's something comforting and intimate about sharing a meal together, whatever the occasion. Whether it's at a coffee shop, at home, or a swanky restaurant, food shared is relationship building somehow. For those date nights, would you be brave enough to throw caution to the wind and simply enjoy? Don't stress over the calories or decline dessert and watch him eat alone. Run tomorrow, have salad for the next two days, whatever it takes, but sometimes you have to live in the moment. As long as date night isn't every single night.

Chapter Five:
Traditions Trade Off

> "...in humility value others above yourselves, not looking to your own interests but each of you to the interests of the others."

Dear daughter, we may have some whacko traditions in our family, but I think you'll find most families have their fair share. Some are passed down from generation to generation and are steeped in deep meaning, whereas others simply evolve and stick around for the fun of it.

Why, oh why do we eat ham sandwiches, pickled onions, and potato chips for Christmas breakfast? Absolutely no idea, but somewhere in my family's past, somebody obviously thought it was a great notion, and now we feel as if we might be excommunicated if we dare veer to pancakes or something delicious. We do have some more humane traditions, which are enjoyable to all, but I sincerely apologize for the breakfast thing.

As newlyweds, you get to decide which traditions you will include and which you will ditch. (I'm okay with you ditching the Christmas breakfast, for the record.) For most of us, we learn as we go, and sometimes get swept up in the frenzy and don't get a say because it's expected of us, but if you have the opportunity to think this through in advance, I say *do it*. Discuss together which crazy options are out of your comfort zones, and which you both wholeheartedly enjoy.

To give you the heads-up, some of us can get very protective over our family traditions. I'm not sure why exactly, maybe it's because it knits us to our heritage and gives us a sense of comfort, especially if we live far away from family. So when you and the husband discuss this topic, make sure you are both well-fed and congenial.

WARNING: it can be a terrific springboard for arguments, so be open-minded and go into this with an understanding heart. You've *both* been severed from your regular family life, and insulting his family's Thanksgiving quirks will break down the conversation as well as him laughing at your Christmas breakfast preferences. Be gracious!

"Do nothing out of selfish ambition or vain conceit. Rather, in humility value others above yourselves, not looking to your own interests but each of you to the interests of the others." Philippians 2:3-4 (NIV)

So here's the tricky part: how to create your own new traditions without offending your spouse or ticking off your whole extended family. This may require some fancy footwork and a truckload of grace. There are usually ways to keep folks reasonably happy, but I would caution you not to wear yourself ragged in an attempt to please everyone all of the time. It's not going to happen. The major issue is that you and your husband are both united and on the same page. If that breaks down, it can get downright ugly.

This is the ideal opportunity to set some boundaries with friends and family. (I realize I am your mother, but I will plough on regardless, speaking also to myself.) Most people usually give newlyweds a bit of space in their first year or so, but that's not always the case. Protect your time fiercely. Don't miss Easter because you were busy racing from one family dinner to another. It's a time to try out some traditions — if they crash and burn, no worries, just don't make the same mistake next time. You'll probably fall into some traditions by accident. Some of our best have been unintentional.

I love our relaxed Christmas Eves after a busy church service, when we eat appies, open gifts (we know will be pajamas), read the Christmas story, and watch a Christmas movie snuggled up, all wonderfully content. Or our chilly Boxing Day walk, or opening birthday presents before breakfast. You'll find your rhythm together and it will be so much fun.

Traditions aren't only for Christmas and the holiday seasons. Some family traditions are simply day-to-day things we do out of habit. For example, something my in-laws did as a family was to eat dinner at the table together every evening. My family tended to be a little more hectic/frantic, but I loved the idea, so we purposed to carry this on with our own children, and it's been the greatest blessing. Conversation, intentional checking-in with each other, sharing, joking, bantering, and waiting for countless hours for the slow eater to finish... it's been priceless!

Talk together about your traditions, make it a fun experience, and remember to be flexible where necessary. This is a great exercise in putting each other first and wanting to make your spouse happy. Look back at special moments from your growing-up years that you would both like to reflect in your brand new family unit.

Here are a few traditions some families like to weave into their calendars:

Family photos — usually at Christmas to send out with cards
Sunday dinner — making it a special meal to come together and connect
Family night — pick one night a week or month to do something fun like movies or games together
Birthday parties or dinner celebrations
Pizza night
Christmas baking — special cookies or squares made only for the festive season
Family reunions
Vacations or weekend getaways
Anniversary celebrations
Christmas movie night

I'll bet the Proverbs 31 wife had a plethora of amazing traditions. Maybe it was dressing her family "in scarlet" when it snowed (verse 21), or giving regularly when "she opens her arms to the poor and extends her hands to the needy" (verse 20). Giving is a wonderful tradition, whether it's sponsoring a child in need, serving at a local shelter, or delivering Christmas cookies to your neighbors. Have fun figuring out your traditions, new little family, and let it be something that draws you ever closer together.

Chapter Six:

Sorry

"A happy marriage is the union of two good forgivers."

This will be the shortest chapter of all. It's just one little word. One little pearl. Sorry.

But let me tell you now, it's one of the most important words in a strong, healthy marriage. It shows vulnerability, admittance of not always being completely right about absolutely everything, a soft heart desiring reconciliation, and a maturity essential in any relationship.

Confession time: I suck at this.

Saying sorry really shouldn't be that hard, but it is. Fortunately for me (and the rest of the family), I am married to a man with a much bigger heart than my own, and he is never too proud/foolish/ pigheaded to apologize for being wrong, even when we've both messed up. Me on the other hand... let's just say I'm a work in progress, far from perfect. Very, very far.

But for you, starting out all fresh and shiny, new in your marriage, I urge you to say sorry to one another. Be sincere, observe his emotions, and notice when he's hurt or when something has truly bothered him. Some guys (and girls) are brick walls and are seemingly unfazed by anything emotional, and may not be very sensitive to your upset state. Others bruise really easily, and a little walking on eggshells may be required until you both figure out what sets off who, and why.

Our Proverbs 31 wife might have struggled inwardly in this area, but she certainly had self-control where it mattered, and as a result she wasn't noted as a proud, unforgiving wife. She was a smart woman, and I have no doubt she was fully able to converse intelligently with her husband, come to agreement or compromise in a timely manner, and I have a feeling she said sorry without too much difficulty.

"She speaks with wisdom, and faithful instruction is on her tongue." (Verse 26)

Something to shoot for, I think!

Throughout our own marriage, we've held to the following 'rule', if you can call it that. It's worked pretty effectively, and has ended any potential brooding fodder, or brewing deep freezes. At the end of the day, no matter what kind of an exhausting, stressful, heartbreaking minefield we have teetered through, we *always* make up before going to sleep. We may not figure out all the answers or have complete closure on a subject, but we do agree that our relationship trumps any other issue, and until we can reach an amicable conclusion, we are at least assured that we still love each other and are willing to work on our differences of opinion.

I am blessed beyond measure to have a compatible husband who dislikes confrontation as much as I do. Almost. We very rarely argue, but over the course of twenty-five years, there have certainly been some "moments", as there will inevitably be for you. It's okay – take a breath, we are all human. How we actually deal with these moments is key.

It's not rocket science figuring out that communication is vital in any relationship, but particularly in a marriage. When one side blows up or shuts down, it's code for "I don't get you." We are different, us women from our men folk. If we're honest, we often don't even understand ourselves (particularly at certain times of the month), so it's tricky business for our husbands as they navigate their way through our complexities. Similarly, guys are a breed unto themselves, and their ways are sometimes beyond comprehension to us girls. What to do?

Clearly, we were created very differently, and on a good day we balance our spouse quite nicely. He washes while we dry, he listens while we talk, he nods while we try on clothing options, and we read the map while he drives (or vice versa). But some days, it all breaks down and simply doesn't work. We're too emotional, he's too emotional, we're frazzled, he's chilled, we're wired, he's tired, and today is certainly not paradise. Snippy, pointed jabs can lead to painful, long-lasting words that insult everyone and everything from his family to your dog. It's not pretty, and nobody wants a relationship like that. It hurts and it's hard work. But in order to dig yourself out from under all that pain, one of you has to say it: "Sorry."

I love this simple, succinct quote by Ruth Bell Graham: "A happy marriage is the union of two good forgivers."

When partner number one has offered that outstretched hand, it's so much easier to forgive, and then say sorry for anything that might have been hurled out there for good measure. I don't wish to belittle forgiveness and apologies, because I realize there are big issues which may take a lot more than a conversation to mend, or even a third party coming in to save the day. I pray your discrepancies will be minuscule, dear daughter, I really do. And that they can be nipped in the bud before you close your eyes and dream of various poisoning methods! Don't go to sleep angry with one another. They are not my words, it is real wisdom from The Word, put there to protect you and give you the very best in life:

"'In your anger do not sin': Do not let the sun go down while you are still angry, and do not give the devil a foothold." Ephesians 4:26-27 (NIV)

Chapter Seven:
Stand By Your Man

"Stand by your man
And show the world you love him
Keep giving all the love you can
Stand by your man"

If you're of a certain age, or at all familiar with country music, you'll probably be doing your best Tammy Wynette rendition of "Stand By Your Man" about now. If you have no idea what I'm talking about, it's worth looking up this classic song, just for kicks. This chapter is an attempt to encourage you, dear daughter, and me, and anyone else who might be reading, to give the men in our lives a little R-E-S-P-E-C-T.

Why do I feel the need to dedicate a whole chapter on this subject? Mainly because I'm a woman and I know what makes us tick, I know how easily frustrated we can become with our husbands, and I know how tempting it is to jump on the proverbial bandwagon and join the masses in berating the male portion of the population.

The obvious fact is: we are very different from our husbands. Quite frankly, it would be a nightmare if they were exactly like us. Can you imagine? We *should* embrace our differences and celebrate our combined strengths, of course, but in real life it can be a hard slog. It takes some of us (me included) a long, long time to actually clue in to why our husbands do what they do. They aren't wrong; they're just peculiar, in a good way.

My issue stemmed from the fact that I grew up with three sisters and an awful lot of estrogen. Other than my dad, my husband was the first solid dose of male I had encountered, and I didn't understand a lot of him. But it didn't bother me particularly, and I loved him to death, so I went with it. Honestly, I'm not proud of the eye rolling, the sarcastic quips, and unfair judgment I doled out, especially early on in our marriage. I don't think it really hit me until I looked around and noticed how ugly that particular brand of wife looked on other women. I didn't want to look like that, or behave like that myself, and I certainly didn't want to demean my husband.

But wait—isn't that how husbands are portrayed in society? Isn't our amusement on TV sitcoms derived from the stupid husbands with foot-in-mouth disease who can't do anything right? In fact, why do we need a husband at all these days? Isn't it kind of old fashioned? Isn't the whole 'submit to your husband' politically incorrect or something?

A potentially nasty can of worms. I really wish I had been encouraged to work through some of these issues years ago, but then again, perhaps they weren't quite as prevalent. Regardless, I believe it's worth taking some time to unravel the importance of standing by your man.

It's in the Bible. "It's in the Bible. Like it or not, we are commanded (not as a joke or a mere suggestion) to submit to our husbands. In the Greek language, the word that is translated as "submit" actually means "umbrella", which is a beautiful picture. To "come under the cover of, be protected by your husband" is why the Bible says that a woman is to submit to her "own" husband, that no other man is to touch her, and that her husband is to take care of her in every way. You are nestled under that umbrella together.

I'm not going to pretend it's easy or that I am expert in this particular field (nowhere near!), but I do know that it helps if the man we are submitting to is treating us correctly...." It makes sense that when our man loves us unconditionally "as Christ loved the church" (Ephesians 5:25), then we will be on the same page, and willing to listen, and wanting the best for our marriage. After all, Christ gave His very life for His beloved, and that manifests an awful lot of love.

The same Bible that tells wives to submit to their husbands, also instructs the husbands to *love* their wives. Multiple times. Submission and love, the two go hand-in-hand and one feeds from the other in an ideal relationship — that's the one we need to strive toward. The flip side is that failure on either part makes the submission and love duet an ugly, vicious cycle. The answer? I'm not going to pretend it's simple, because it's something you will work on throughout your whole married life, but if you're both in agreement that Scripture is truth, then that's where you need to return. Both of you.

"However, each one of you also must love his wife as he loves himself, and the wife must respect her husband." Ephesians 5:33 (NIV)

I must be a horribly slow learner, because, for me, it took years and years to see a glimpse of the why's and wherefore's of my own husband. It

45

really wasn't until I had the boys, your glorious little brothers, that I began receiving small revelations on man/boy behaviors, and realizing it was completely natural. I have to give some of the thanks to a marvelous book, *Bringing Up Boys* by James C. Dobson, which touches on the somewhat confused role of men in society today. It gave me insight not only in raising my little boys, but I had many "Ah-ha!" moments when I discovered interesting facts about my husband, too. A definite recommended read.

Your marriage is a partnership, not a one-upmanship, and if you do your part in supporting your man whenever possible, you won't regret it. Be counter-cultural and hold your husband in high esteem. Let other's know you love and respect him – your actions will speak volumes, but your words go a really long way, too. Give him words of encouragement and affirmation; let him know you're in his corner. Always.

Before you go thinking I'm asking you to be old-fashioned, apron-wearing doormat, let me assure you that when you stand by your man, you are being strong. You see, it's not always easy and it may cause you to shake off a layer of pride and you won't get it right every single time. But if you do respect him, you'll glean respect from others watching, and he will love you all the more for it. I'm a work-in-progress, but when I read about our Proverbs 31 woman, who was far from weak and certainly nobody's doormat, I want this—her love, strength and confidence pours from her life directly over to her husband's, and as a result he is respected by all.

"Her husband is respected at the city gate, where he takes his seat among the elders of the land." Proverbs 31:23 (NIV)

You are a couple now, dear daughter, and you expect your new husband to be supportive, to be by your side and fight in your corner for the rest of your lives. Can he expect the same from you? Start your marriage off on the right foot, and you'll dance more often.

"Stand by your man
And show the world you love him
Keep giving all the love you can
Stand by your man"
(Tammy Wynette/ Billy Sherrill)

Chapter Eight:
Super-husband Syndrome

"Better to live in a desert than with a quarrelsome and nagging wife."

What happens after your Cinderella wedding carriage returns to being a pumpkin?

After the highs of engagement and wedding, it's only natural to experience a little 'coming down to earth' together. Whether you ease yourselves into it gracefully, or instantly deflate like a popped balloon, is pretty much up to the two of you. So, dear daughter, let me offer some pearls to soften the blow and sweeten the transition a little.

Newsflash: Your husband is not a superhero. You are now either rolling your eyes and saying, "Duh!" or clutching your heart, completely mortified that I should even suggest his lack of powers. Truth is, even if we don't admit it, we all put our husbands on the superhero pedestal. Even the strongest, most independent among us expect him to step up and perform the impossible.

When we dream of being married, we long for a perfect partner. We anticipate he will be most, if not all, of the following: communicative, a good listener, reliable, spontaneous, strong, gentle, a good provider, generous, romantic, attentive, understanding, sensitive, punctual, funny, charming, and never late home for dinner. Is that too much to ask? Well, yes. Especially all at the same time and especially for a poor, unsuspecting, newlywed husband.

Hopefully, you will be a very understanding wife with realistic expectations, but many of us go into marriage thinking our fresh-faced groom will anticipate our every mood swing, read our minds, and accommodate our wifely wishes with his cape flapping in the breeze.

For Christians, there is even the danger of putting him in the place of Jesus, and that's scary. Our husband is the one we run to, confide in, draw strength from, and share our fears, hopes, and dreams with. He probably doesn't even know it, but we can unintentionally put him on a par with the Almighty, and that's certainly not fair. Your man is incredibly human, as are you. He's not going to ever be perfect in this life, so maybe ease up on the pressure pedal. I'm completely guilty of this, and then I remember to look at myself and how "godlike" I am (not). Then I look at my true Savior, Jesus, and see that He's the only One who meets my every need. My husband is here to share the journey, share the love, to share the laughter and pain along the way. But we BOTH need a Savior, and it is definitely not each other!

"Better to live in a desert than with a quarrelsome and nagging wife." Proverbs 21:19 (NIV)

Oh my. A desert? That's pretty extreme, which must mean it really is *that* bad. I came across this little gem recently, and it gave me cause to pause. I was familiar with another verse earlier in this Proverb, the one where it's better to live on the corner of a roof than with a nagging wife — I would often have a chuckle about that one, but this desert comparison was new to me, and somewhat disturbing.

Barren, dry, scorching, blistering heat, dying from thirst, and this is preferable to living with a moody woman? Contentious, angry, quarrelsome, fretful, nagging — these are all words used to describe this horrific battleaxe. What kind of woman is she? Who would marry her in the first place? Scary answer: We all have the potential to be that woman.

That's why it's written in Scripture. Every verse is there for a reason, and I can't help noticing there are a few about the nagging wife in Proverbs. Maybe it's because Solomon wrote the book and he had something like seven hundred wives and three hundred concubines — that's over one thousand women in his life! Or maybe it's actually there as a tool for our marriage.

In Proverbs 31, we see that "nagging battleaxe" is not on the description list for this wife. No, instead Verse 12 says, "She brings him good, not harm, all the days of her life." Smart lady.

None of us would *choose* to be a nagger. Personally, I absolutely hate hearing myself nag anyone about anything. This often results in me doing it all myself instead of asking (and re-asking) for help. Not ideal. In a perfect world, you would ask your darling once to pick up his socks/put down the toilet seat/not put empty packets back in the cupboard, but it's simply not going to happen. Here's the thing — what's important or irritating to you might not be important or irritating to him. It will likely not even be on his radar. So you have to choose between these options:

1. Communicate with him. Tell him you don't *want* to nag. Tell him the things that are important to you and why. Ask him what his peeves are, too. It works both ways.

2. Pick your battles. If there is something that has the potential to be an exploding point for you, and you're sick of the sound of your own voice (I was going to say "you are sounding like your mother", but I am writing this to my daughter and it physically hurts to say that!), then find neutral ground. He insists on squeezing the toothpaste tube from the middle instead of the bottom? Have two separate tubes and take a breath. The socks can't quite make it to the laundry pile? Maybe a little laundry hamper is required in his closet. Again, this works both ways, so listen to the things he has to repeat and get all agitated about, and see if you can find a solution. A great deal of nagging is about the fluffy stuff.

3. Buy him some sun block and a one-way ticket to the Sahara. Just kidding. But it might be a good idea to keep a bottle of sun block somewhere handy where you can see it, just as a little reminder to yourself.

You are not Superman and Wonder Woman, and nobody expects that from either of you, so don't put the pressure on each other. You are simply Mr. & Mrs., and that's pretty super in my mind!

Chapter Nine:
What's Yours Is Mine!

"For better, for worse, for richer, for poorer…"

Ah, those famous wedding vows! With love-struck adoration, the couple makes this bold statement to one another, but I wonder how many fresh young brides really think deeply about the words they utter at the altar. We have no way of knowing what the future will hold in our years as husband and wife, so it's a huge step of faith to make these promises. You probably imagine yourselves in your twilight years as a content, elderly couple in matching rocking chairs on the porch watching the sunset. I hope and pray that will be the case, but your journey there could be one of economic gymnastics.

I don't know how you feel as a new bride about to 'half own' or have 'joint custody' of all your husband's stuff, but I remember feeling a little uncomfortable. Don't get me wrong, I had the good side of the deal as my darling is the sensible one, but it took a little time to get used to thinking of his stuff as mine. I'd never owned my own car, and suddenly there it was. Mine. I would imagine it must be increasingly difficult to meld possessions for those getting married later in life, but even the little items can be bones of contention when it comes to sharing.

Stuff. He uses your special fluffy towel, he breaks one your favorite mugs, and he eats the last of your chocolate cookies. A few deep, cleansing breaths are in order. You may have to look at this sharing business from his perspective, too. He uses the fluffy towel because it's the only one left in the closet, the mug toppled out of the cupboard due to the stack of miscellaneous mugs you don't have the heart to throw out because they're sentimental, and the unlabelled chocolate cookies are pretty much fair game in the pantry.

Sharing. You had a taste of it with your siblings, and it was tough even then. As toddlers we squabble, as teenagers we argue, and then as adults we marry and jump into a state of perpetual sharing. It's not always easy. The wonderful thing about wedding gifts is that they are bought for you as a married couple. The toaster enters your kitchen wrapped in shiny paper with a big white bow via Great Aunt Maude and you're good to go. You both feel comfortable using that toaster whenever you desire. But when it comes to using money from your new husband's bank account for those shoes you desperately ~~want~~ need...

Money. The source of many an argument within any relationship, but especially in marriage. I'd love to be able to tell you this is something you'll sort out in the first year and then be fine forevermore, but the truth is, life throws you all sorts of curve balls and your circumstances will most likely change several times before you reach that cozy rocking chair on the porch.

The first place of discomfort I remember was my new husband's bank account. It didn't seem right, me being able to siphon funds from his hard-earned cash to buy things — even if those things included food he was going to consume and a winter jacket he would wear. We discovered the best way for us to handle our finances was to have three separate accounts: one in my name, one in his name, and a joint account for us to manage together. We were both earning salaries, so our pay went into our individual accounts, and we would transfer a sum from both into the joint account each month. That jar was a lot more comfortable to dip into for both of us, and still left me with a sense of independence should I need to make an occasional purchase (the shoes). Twenty-five years later, we still have delightful budget conversations and juggle funds to make things work for us. But I'm grateful for always having a little account of my very own, even if it's permanently depleted.

Accountability. Don't you just love the ring of that word? Answerability, blameworthiness, liability... hardly romantic in a book about marriage, but it's a reality on several levels. Financial accountability is key between you and your spouse. Secrets of any description between you are a corrosive, festering sore, and money secrets never, ever turn out well. I urge you to start out with complete transparency when it comes to your finances. Don't withhold bills, credit card debt information, or mistakes you make with your money.

The fact of the matter is, you might have very different thoughts and convictions when it comes to your finances, and although you should already have had initial discussions before getting married, it won't become a reality until you're in the thick of it — paying bills, making purchases, and trying to save.

It's fairly common to see a couple comprised of a spender and a saver (no prizes for guessing which one I am!) I like to think it balances everything out in a perfect world, but it can also be a huge headache. You'll have to figure out how to navigate your particular money ship, but here are a few tips, which might help to ease the seas:

1. Have a spending limit where you need to consult your other half before making a purchase — you *both* have to adhere to this.
2. Balance your books regularly. Be on the same page and make sure you both know what's coming in and going out each month, and keep an eye on it.
3. Be proactive — when you know additional expenses will be incurred (Christmas, vacations etc.), make provision for it, save a little in advance to avoid the migraine of massive bills afterwards.
4. Discretionary funds — even if it's a few dollars per week, allow yourselves a little slack money to spend as a 'freebie'.
5. Giving — agree at the outset what your giving to the church or charitable donations will be.
6. Be realistic when making a budget, work together on it, and make sure you are both on board.

It's vitally important to talk about money with your husband. It's not always pretty and you might disagree and have to work through some issues, but as with every aspect of your marriage, communication is golden. Find a time and a place for discussion where you will *both* be congenial and open. Go out together for coffee with your laptop or spread out your bills on the kitchen table, whatever works for you. Timing is everything however — if one of you comes alive at the thought of spreadsheets and has the uncanny ability to talk nitty-gritty numbers late at night, you might want to check in on your partner, because bedtime might not be budget time in their book. I speak from experience.

On your journey, you may both find yourselves in 'support mode' at various times, financially as well as emotionally, toward one another. In our case, I supported while he retrained and qualified in his profession, and then he supported while I chose to stay home and home school, and now he supports me in my writing, and I'm there to take the slack when his business is consuming. It's not a race and we don't begrudge each other's accomplishments or financial needs. It's this love-partnership, and you need to be each other's best cheerleader.

So, sharing isn't only a matter for your finances and possessions, dear daughter. You have a wonderful husband who you will share so much with over the years; love, time, interests, thoughts, faith, tears, joy, children, grandchildren, and eventually, that sunset and the porch with the matching rocking chairs.

Chapter Ten:
Happily Ever After

"It always protects, always trusts, always hopes, always perseveres. Love never fails…"

As you set sail on the voyage as man and wife, your father and I celebrate twenty-five years of marriage. We have gleaned a lot through experience, from watching others, and from attempting to follow what the Bible has to say about this unique and wonderful relationship. I hope to learn a lot more in the next twenty-five years.

We have had some excellent role models around us to show us that marriage *is* for life and it's a truly precious gift. I urge you, dear daughter, to surround yourselves with couples who *love* being married. They are easy to spot. Glean from them what you can, and allow them to pour into your lives. Many couples struggle, and you need to be a support and encouragement to them for sure, but if you find yourself in the company of unhappy wives everywhere you turn, it's not going to help your relationship.

Keep a balance, and ensure you have friends who will rejoice with you in your happiness and squeal when your husband brings you flowers. Don't be dragged down by the cynical friend in a ghastly relationship who quips that your flowers are lame and a total waste of money. Be protective of your marriage, and never, ever be apologetic for being happily married.

I don't claim to have a miraculous formula for an awesome marriage, but I do have three practical 'L's, which have helped me immensely, and I think they might be beneficial for you, too:

LAUGH — often and together. A sense of humor is sometimes all that keeps us sane, and I can't imagine going through marriage without it. Loosen up and lighten up — you'll make mistakes, both of you, but if you have the ability to laugh about it together, it'll make everything so much more bearable. You burned dinner again? Serve the cremated offering with a cheeky grin and let him guess what it was. Then order take-out. He burned dinner again? Another grin, another guessing game, another take-out. It's all good. Don't get all defensive and don't make him eat something you wouldn't feed the dog. Trust me, in the big scheme of things, it's no biggie and you can laugh at it.

Have fun together. Remember the pre-engagement, stress-free days of dating? You can claim them back now. Plus, you're actually married so there's no curfew, no pressure, no need to impress him (because he's seen you at 5am sans make-up and he still loves you!) Do things that make you laugh — hang out with humorous friends, go to a hilarious movie, roll down a sand dune, or go tobogganing. Don't let everything be serious in your relationship. If all else fails, start a tickle fight to lighten the mood. You never know where that might lead.

LIVE — in constant communication. You know this. Everyone knows this: communication is key. We *know* it, but we don't always act on it. And quite often, it's not until the communication is almost non-existent that we realize there's an issue. It may be hard to imagine right now, you lovely young bride, with thoughts centered on your 'couple-ness' and still basking in the light of your wedding day. But one morning you might wake up and realize your life is starting to veer in a slightly different direction to your husband's.

It could be that work is consuming you (or him), or that you suddenly feel the urge to start a family and that's all you can think about (or he starts getting broody), or you are spending more time with friends than with your man, or that it's never just the two of you alone. Conversation is stilted at best, you can't remember the last romantic date you went on, and you can barely smile at him, let alone laugh with him. More often than not, the cause for most of this is a break down in communication, and it starts small.

There's something cute and comforting about the two of you nestled on the sofa reading your separate books, or perusing cyberspace on your laptops. You're together, you don't feel the need to constantly talk; the silence is comfortable between you, and that's absolutely fine. But watch out for alarm bells; you get up and make your own drinks separately without offering to serve one another, you start eating at different times from each other due to 'schedules', you don't greet each other or say goodbye as you leave for the day, and before you know it, you can't remember when you last conversed together. Bad communication is not always a hostile issue caused by a massive wedge between you. Sometimes it sneaks up gradually without you even noticing.

You may hear 'empty nesters' bemoan the fact that they have to get used to their spouse again now that all the kids have left home. Sadly, on occasion it's too much effort and results in the marriage, (which had evidently been held together by the kids), finally dissolving. It's heartbreaking, but another reminder for us to keep working at our marriages, no matter how long we've been together. Communicate well, dear daughter, and if you start strong and maintain due diligence throughout your life as a wife, then you'll always have your best friend sleeping right next to you.

"Be completely humble and gentle; be patient, bearing with one another in love. Make every effort to keep the unity of the Spirit through the bond of peace." Ephesians 4:2-4 (NIV)

LOVE — keep the romance alive! This is definitely a biggie in my book. Many years ago, on retuning from our honeymoon, we attended a Christian conference in South Wales, and the main speaker was Josh McDowell, a Christian apologist, evangelist, and writer. He was from America, and rather a big name in Christian circles, so we were keen to meet him in person after the event. There we were, deeply tanned from two weeks in Cyprus, stars in our eyes and love written all over our faces, all excited to meet this man. We chatted with him briefly, and explained we had recently come back from our honeymoon. His reply stuck with us both evermore (and I remember very little, ever, so this in itself is a small miracle). He said, "Never come off your honeymoon, kids. My wife and I have been married many years, and we never came off our honeymoon. It's the best advice I can give you."
He was still giddily, happily married after a

hefty amount of time, and this was what he put it down to. Oh, I know there are various components to a good, healthy marriage, but remaining in 'honeymoon mode' is superb advice. Realistically, this doesn't mean drinks with tiny umbrellas on your loungers in the dining room every evening, and you are probably going to have to go to work and communicate with the outside world fairly regularly.

But I think he was getting at is this: that glow, that adoration you have for one another when you are newly wed — hang onto it with a vice grip. Remember what attracted you to your spouse in the first place and don't make it your mission to change him. Make time for one another, maintain that desire to serve one another and want the very best for him. Remember everything love is, and put it into practice.

"Love is patient, love is kind. It does not envy, it does not boast, it is not proud. It does not dishonor others, it is not self-seeking, it is not easily angered, it keeps no record of wrongs. Love does not delight in evil but rejoices with the truth. It always protects, always trusts, always hopes, always perseveres. Love never fails..." 1 Corinthians 13: 4-8 (NIV)

It wasn't terribly hard to live this out on your honeymoon, when all was rosy and romance was on full beam. But these are verses to take into every day, sometimes they will be near impossible to stick to, but the good news is, you're not alone. Firstly, we are all human and every one of us struggles to live this kind of love, especially with our spouse. Secondly, and more importantly, we have a Heavenly

Father who *is* love, and He promises to never leave us or forsake us. It's a precious promise to take us through all our days as man and wife.

So, how to keep the romance alive? It's not going to happen magically all on its own, so it's yet another area requiring commitment and effort. But it's the fun one! Be sure to go on 'real' dates together (the grocery store does not count), plan vacations together, compliment one another, schedule alone time as a couple with no other distractions, buy little gifts to surprise each other, invest in candles, hold hands a lot, and find out what *he* thinks is romantic — you may be surprised.

One other thing, your husband (I'm sure) didn't marry you purely for your looks, even though you are completely beautiful. Anyone who only looks at the outer shell is considered shallow, and rightly so. But I want to throw something out there — you can take or leave it. The thing is, most husbands enjoy their wives who look their best. I'm not condoning plastic surgery here, merely suggesting running a brush through your hair and dressing nicely for him once in a while (or every day, if you so wish!)

There are probably some guys who don't mind either way, but generally I think I'm safe in saying a man appreciates it when we go to the effort of looking 'nice'. Before you slam the book shut, let me say that it works both ways, doesn't it? Wouldn't you be a tad disappointed if he wore sweats and a three-day beard growth out for your anniversary dinner? And forgot to wear deodorant? I thought so. I'm not implying you need to vacuum the living room in stilettos or anything, but maybe shave your legs and don a frock every so often? Before I move on from this little rant, one last thing: compliments go a *really* long way. For both of you.

In saying all this, we know that true beauty comes from within, and there's no use primping and painting a battleaxe. I know your husband will appreciate your kind, generous, loving spirit more than any designer outfit, and in twenty-five years time, that's what will really count. (Although you can still look good!)

"Charm is deceptive, and beauty is fleeting; but a woman who fears the LORD is to be praised." Proverbs 31:30 (NIV)

So, here we are, at the end of the chapter and the end of this 'letter'. I hope there is something here for you, some pearls of wisdom you will find helpful and useful in your new role as a young wife. It's been a privilege to share my thoughts and share my heart, dear daughter. For you, and any other daughters who have read these words, I pray God's richest blessing over your marriage. I pray you will find the deepest love, joy, and peace with your wonderful new husband; surmounted only by the love, joy, and peace you will both find in God Himself.

With love always,
Mum

30567590R00038

Made in the USA
Charleston, SC
17 June 2014